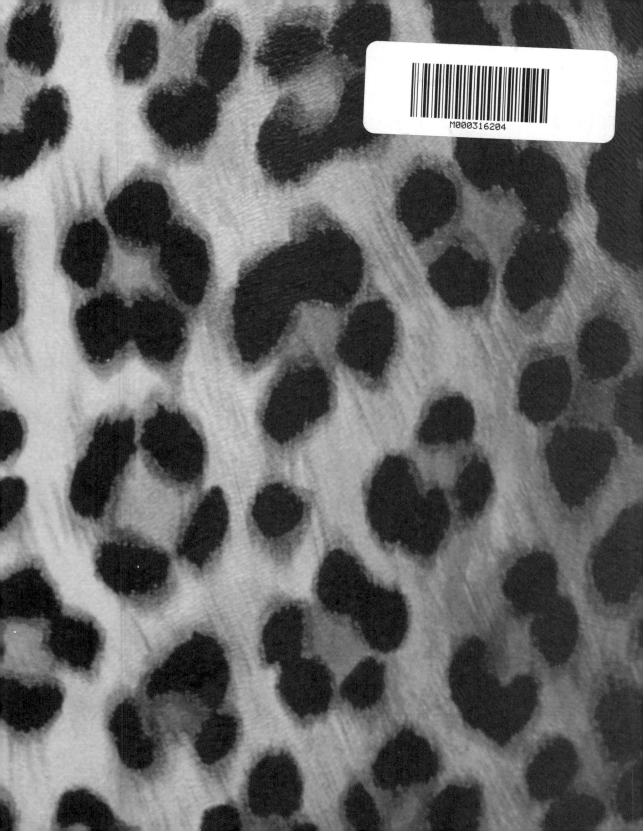

First published in March 2011 by
B. Dutton Publishing Limited, The Grange,
Hones Yard, Farnham, Surrey, GU9 8BB.
Copyright: Jan Clement-May 2011
ISBN-13: 978-1-905113-20-0
All rights reserved.
Reprinted in August 2011

Publisher: Beverley Dutton
Editor: Jenny Stewart
Art Director/Designer: Sarah Ryan
Deputy Editor: Jenny Royle
Designer: Zena Manicom
Sub Editor/Graphic Designer: Louise Pepé
PR and Advertising Manager: Natalie Bull
Photography: Alister Thorpe
Printed in China
Wallpapers supplied by wallpaperdirect.co.uk

Acknowledgements

I would like to say a big thank you, once
again, to Bev and Rob for the opportunity
to publish my work in modelling. It's a huge
passion of mine.

To the production team, Jenny and Sarah,
and Alister for the wonderful photography
throughout the book – keep up the great work.

Dedication

To my husband, Ian, for putting up with endless boxes of cakes and models scattered around
the house and living in organised chaos on a daily basis.

introduction

Modelling is a passion of mine – I can often be found sitting quietly, playing with Sugar Dough and making figures and animals for cakes, cookies and cupcakes. A model on top of a cake or cookie can really add some fun and character to an otherwise simple design.

This book will help you with the basic techniques for modelling animals, from simple creatures of the sea through to the more intricate of dinosaurs. I've found that Sugar Dough is a great medium for modelling – it holds its shape so needs minimum support, has a fantastically smooth finish and tastes good, too. Practise modelling pieces again and again until you're happy with the final result – this will give you confidence in handling the paste as well as the tools and equipment. If it goes wrong, knead it all together and try again!

I hope you have lots of fun making the animal models in this book. If you can involve the children as well, even better – watch their faces light up when they have finished their very own edible animals!

contents

recipes

Once you've made your sugar animals you can display them on a celebration cake, on cupcakes or even on cookies. I've suggested a cake, cupcake or cookie idea for each of the themes in the book, or you can create your own treats to suit the occasion.

Sponge Cake

Ingredients	15cm (6") round	20.5cm (8") round	12 cupcakes/28 mini
Soft margarine	175g (6oz)	225g (8oz)	115g (4oz)
Caster sugar	175g (6oz)	225g (8oz)	115g (4oz)
Baking powder	8ml (1½tsp)	10ml (2tsp)	5ml (1tsp)
Self-raising flour	225g (8oz)	275g (10oz)	115g (4oz)
Eggs	3	5	2
Milk	25ml (1½tbsp)	30ml (2tbsp)	N/A
Baking time	30 minutes	40 minutes	18-20/12-15 minutes

Variations

Chocolate sponge: add 45ml (3tbsp) of good quality cocoa powder to 60ml (4tbsp) of hot, boiled water and mix. Allow to cool before adding to the cake mixture.

Lemon sponge: add the rind of 2 lemons and 60ml (4tbsp) of lemon juice to the cake mixture.

Orange sponge: add the rind of 2 oranges and 60ml (4tbsp) of orange juice to the cake mixture.

Coffee sponge: add 30ml (2tbsp) of coffee essence to the cake mixture.

Sponge cake method

1 Preheat the oven to 180°C/350°F/gas mark 4. Grease the cake tin(s) and line the base with greaseproof paper or baking parchment. Cut a length of greaseproof paper or baking parchment to fit all the way around the inside of the tin(s).

2 Place all the ingredients into a mixing bowl and beat together in a mixer for approximately 2 minutes (or mix by hand) until well blended. Pour the mixture into the prepared tin(s) and level the top.

3   Bake in the preheated oven for the specified time, or until the cake is firm to the touch and has shrunk away from the sides of the tin. Leave to cool in the tin(s) before turning out onto a cooling rack. Allow to cool completely before decorating.

Cupcake method

1   Preheat the oven to 200°C/400°F/gas mark 6. Place the cupcake cases into a 12-hole bun tin.

2   Place all the ingredients into a mixing bowl and beat together in a mixer for 2 minutes (or mix by hand) until well blended. Half-fill the cake cases with the cake mixture and level the tops.

3   Bake in the preheated oven for around 18-20 minutes, or until the cakes have risen and are firm to the touch. Remove the cakes from the bun tin and leave to cool on a cooling rack.

Mini cupcake method

1   Preheat the oven to 200°C/400°F/gas mark 6. Place the cupcake cases into 24-hole mini tart tins.

2   Place all the ingredients into a mixing bowl and beat together in a mixer for 2 minutes (or mix by hand) until well blended. Half-fill the cake cases with the cake mixture and level the tops.

3   Bake in the preheated oven for around 12-15 minutes, or until the cakes have risen and are firm to the touch. Remove the cakes from the tart tin and leave to cool on cooling racks.

Buttercream

Makes around 625g (1lb 6oz) of buttercream, enough for a 20.5cm (8") cake.

175g (6oz) margarine or unsalted butter, softened
450g (1lb) icing sugar, sifted
10ml (2tsp) milk
5ml (1tsp) vanilla essence

1   Put the margarine or butter in a mixer (or mix by hand) and beat until it appears lighter in colour. Add the vanilla essence and sifted icing sugar, a little at a time. Blend all the icing sugar and milk gradually until it becomes a light and fluffy mix.

2   To store, place in an airtight container and refrigerate. Use within 10 days. Bring to room temperature and mix again before use.

Cookies

175g (6oz) butter
55g (2oz) caster sugar
225g (8oz) self-raising flour, sifted
Cutters or templates
Baking trays, lightly greased
Wire cooling rack

1   Preheat the oven to 180°C/350°F/gas mark 4. Cream the butter and the caster sugar together until light and creamy. Gradually add the sifted self-raising flour, then knead together lightly.

2   Roll out the dough to a thickness of 5mm (¼") and cut out an assortment of shapes using templates or cutters. Place on the greased baking trays and bake for 8-10 minutes until pale brown. Leave to cool on a wire rack.

equipment and edibles

The checklists below are the basic 'toolkit' for all the modelling, cake covering and cookie decorating projects throughout this book. Additional items are included at the beginning of each one if anything extra is needed, as are the specific colours and quantities of pastes. Some tools will be used far more than others but all are essential for achieving good quality results in your edible artwork.

Covering cakes

(1) Cupcake cases (2) Icing sugar shaker (3) Marzipan (4) Non-stick board, large (5) Ribbon
(6) Rolling pin, large (7) Sharp knife (8) Smoother (9) Sugarpaste

Modelling

1. Bone tool
2. Cake cards
3. Cocktail sticks
4. Cranked palette knife
5. Dresden tool
6. Edible glue (SK)
7. Food pens (SK)
8. Non-stick board, small
9. Paintbrushes: nos. 1 and 2
10. Rolling pin, small
11. Scissors
12. Spaghetti (raw)
13. Straws
14. Sugar Dough (SK)
15. White vegetable fat

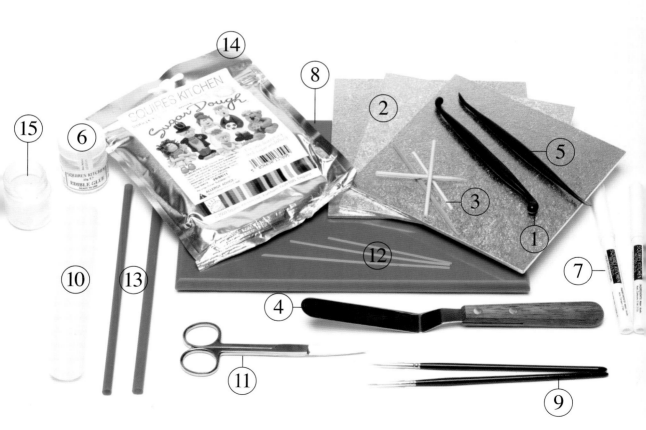

modelling basics

Sugar Dough is easy to use and is ideal for modelling animals and figures. These basic hints and tips will ensure you get brilliant results every time!

- There are just a few basic shapes in modelling which can then be made into almost anything.

1 The ball: roll the paste in the middle of your hands firmly to prevent cracking.

2 The sausage: first, roll the paste into a ball then roll back and forwards on a work surface to lengthen. Roll just a little to make a short, fat sausage or continue rolling to make a longer, thinner sausage.

3 The cone: first, roll the paste into a ball. Place onto a work surface then cup your hands around the ball and turn the paste back and forth. The paste will have a flat base from sitting on the surface and the top should come to a point between your hands.

From these shapes you can make teardrops, pear shapes, discs or tapered sausages as needed for your sugar models.

● Rub a little white vegetable fat into your hands before kneading Sugar Dough: this makes it more pliable and less likely to crack, giving a more, professional finish to your work. It also prevents the stronger colours from sticking to your hands when working the paste and helps to create an even consistency when adding colour to the paste.

● Wash your hands in warm, soapy water between colour changes and keep your tools clean at all times to prevent small pieces of paste from transferring onto other colours. Make sure that your hands are completely dry before handling the paste otherwise it will become sticky.

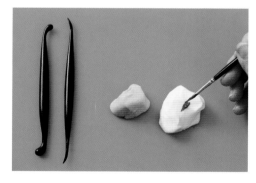

● Use SK Edible Glue to stick pieces together. Using a paintbrush, apply a little glue to the surface of the Sugar Dough before working on the next piece to allow the glue to go tacky. To stick the pieces together, hold them in position and support if necessary until they are held together securely. Working in this way should save you time.

● If you would like to try working with different flavours, you can use marzipan or Cocoform (modelling chocolate) instead of Sugar Dough. Add paste food colours to create all the colours you need. As both types of paste are very soft, you may not need to use edible glue to stick pieces together.

AQUATICS

From enormous whales of the deep sea to friendly frogs from the garden pond, aquatic creatures are bright, colourful and great fun to make.

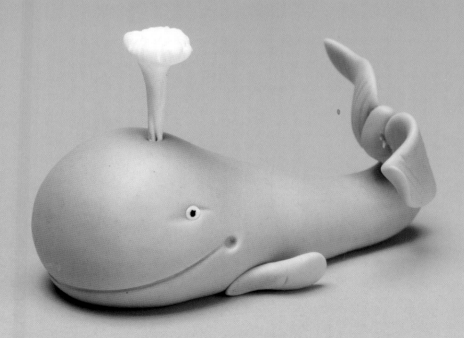

goldfish

edibles

SK Sugar Dough: 60g (2oz)
Orange, pinch of Yellow

SK Food Colour Pen: Black

1 For the body of the goldfish, shape 50g of Orange Sugar Dough into a cone. Mark a line on each side and at the top of the head with a Dresden tool. Push the end of a bone tool into the paste to create the eye sockets and mark scales all over the fish's body with a drinking straw at a 45° angle. Indent the underside of the body at the front with a Dresden tool, coming up around 5mm from the base.

2 Make 2 front side fins using 1g of paste for each one. Shape each one into a pear shape, flatten slightly and mark with a Dresden tool. Secure to the body with a little edible glue. Repeat the same process with the back fins.

3 For the top fin, roll a small ball (approximately 2g) of paste into a sausage 3.5cm long. Flatten slightly, mark with a Dresden tool and secure to the top of the body with edible glue.

4 Pinch a small amount of paste from the remaining 5g, roll into a small sausage shape and bend downwards slightly at each end to make the upper lip. Secure to the front

of the head and make an incision with a small, sharp knife for the mouth.

5 Use the rest of the paste to shape a tail, mark both sides with a Dresden tool and secure to the back end of the body.

6 Roll 2 small balls from Yellow Sugar Dough, brush a small amount of edible glue into the eye sockets and attach each eyeball. Push the end of a Black Food Colour Pen into each of the eyes for the pupils.

frog

edibles

SK Sugar Dough: 45g (1½oz) Green, 3g (pinch) White

SK Food Colour Pen: Black

Important note: Remember to remove the spaghetti before the model is eaten.

1 Divide the Green Sugar Dough as follows: 18g for the body; 10g for the head; 4 x 3g for the legs; and 1g for the eyes.

2 Roll the body into a ball and push a 4cm (1½") long piece of dried spaghetti down through the middle of the body to help support the head.

3 Reserve a pinch of White Sugar Dough for the eyes, then shape the remaining white paste into a bib and attach to the front of the frog's body with a little edible glue.

4 Roll out each of the legs into equal sausage lengths, pinch between your finger and thumb at one end and then make two incisions with a small, sharp knife for the toes. Smooth over the cut edges and spread them apart. Bend the back legs back on themselves and secure to the sides of the body with edible glue. Secure the front legs in place and bring them round to the front slightly.

5 Roll the head into a ball and mark the mouth with a Dresden tool. Brush a little edible glue around the exposed spaghetti and ease the head into place.

6 Roll the eyes in green paste, roll the reserved white paste into 2 small balls and push the white paste into the green. Roll once again to make neat balls and attach to the top of the frog's head with a little edible glue. Draw a line down each of the eyes using a Black Food Colour Pen.

octopus

edibles

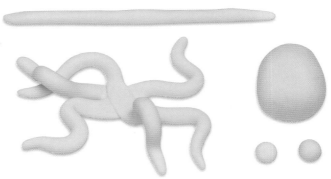

SK Sugar Dough: 100g (3½oz) Yellow

SK Food Colour Pen: Black

1 Divide the yellow paste as follows: 2g for the eyes; 38g for the head; and 4 x 15g for the legs.

2 Roll out 4 equal lengths for the legs and lay them over each other to form a star. Secure in the centre using edible glue.

3 Roll the head into an oval shape and secure to the centre of the legs with a little edible glue. Push the end of a paintbrush into the head to make a mouth opening.

4 Roll the eyes into small balls and secure to the top of the head with edible glue. Push a Black Food Colour Pen into the centre of both for the pupils.

5 Curl the legs around each other randomly. Bring 2 opposite ends up to the top of the head and secure with a little edible glue.

crab

edibles

SK Sugar Dough: 15g (½oz) Orange
SK Food Colour Pen: Black

1 Divide the paste as follows: 6g for the head; a small pinch for each of the eyes; 2g for each of the front claws; and 3 x 1g for the legs.

2 Roll a tapered sausage for each of the legs, making the centre leg slightly longer than the other 2. Pinch the 3 legs together at the centre.

3 Shape the front claws and make an incision into each one. Open up the claws slightly and secure to the front of the legs.

4 Roll the head into a ball then slightly flatten between your finger and thumb along one edge. Mark the mouth opening with the blunt side of a small knife and push the end of a paintbrush into either end of the mouth to create large dimples. Secure the head to the top of the legs with edible glue.

5 Roll a small ball for each of the eyes and secure to the top of the head with a little edible glue. Mark the eyeballs with a Black Food Colour Pen.

shark

edibles

SK Sugar Dough: 3g (pinch) Black, 75g (2½oz) White

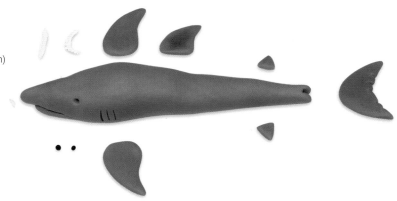

1 Before mixing the 2 colours together, take off a small amount of each and reserve for later. Mix together the remaining Black and White Sugar Dough to make a grey colour and divide as follows: 1g for the top fin; 2 x 3g for the side front fins; a small pinch for the back side fins; 6g for the tail; and the remaining for the body.

2 Model an elongated cone shape for the body and bring the head end to a rounded point for the nose. Cut an incision with a small, sharp knife for the mouth and make another small incision at the tail end to help hold the tail in place. Push the end of a paintbrush into the head twice to make the eye sockets. Using a small knife, mark 3 lines alongside where the side fins will go on both sides of the body for the gills.

3 Shape the front side fins and attach in place with a small amount of edible glue. Repeat with the smaller side fins at the back and the top fin. Shape the tail into a crescent shape, make small incisions using a

small, sharp knife and secure in the incision made earlier for a neat finish.

4 Roll 2 small lengths of white paste for the rows of teeth and mark each length with a Dresden tool to look like jagged teeth. Open the shark's mouth slightly and secure the teeth inside the mouth with a little edible glue. Remove any excess paste if they are too long.

5 Push the end of the Dresden tool into the nose area to make 2 nostrils. Roll the reserved Black Sugar Dough into 2 small balls, brush a little edible glue in each of the eye sockets and push the paste into place for the eyes.

whale

edibles

SK Sugar Dough: 5g (just under ¼oz)
Blue, 105g (3¾oz) White

SK Food Colour Pen: Black

Important note: Remember to remove the spaghetti before the model is eaten.

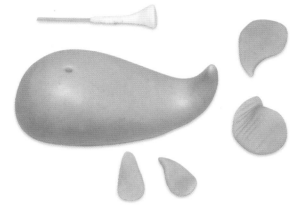

1 Reserve 5g of White Sugar Dough for the eyes and spout. Mix together the remaining White and Blue Sugar Dough to make pale blue. Divide the paste for the whale as follows: 2 x 1g for the front fins; 2 x 2g (pinch) for the tail; and the remaining for the body.

2 Model the body into a pear shape, elongate the tail end and bend upwards. Mark the mouth with the blunt side of a small knife and make dimples with a bone tool. Push the bone tool into the paste above the mouth on each side of the head and drag the tool towards the tail to make the eye sockets. Push a paintbrush handle into the top of the head for the spout to fit into later.

3 Shape the front fins and bend into shape. Secure to the sides of the body with a little edible glue. Shape the tail fins, mark both sides with the blunt edge of a small knife and secure to the tail end with edible glue, holding in position until secure.

4 Roll 2 tiny balls of White Sugar Dough for the eyes, brush a little edible glue in the eye sockets and secure in place. Push a Black Food Colour Pen into the eyes for the pupils.

5 For the spout, dip the end of a 5cm (2") piece of dried spaghetti into edible glue and tease the remaining white paste about 2cm down the spaghetti. Widen and shape the top of the paste and mark with a Dresden tool. Push the length of uncovered spaghetti into the opening and mark the White Sugar Dough with the Dresden tool.

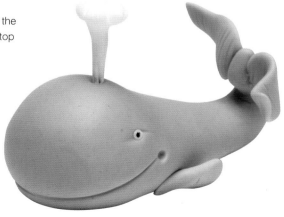

eel

edibles

SK Sugar Dough: 50g (1¾oz)
Golden Bear Brown, 1g (tiny
pinch) White

SK Food Colour Pen: Black

1 Reserve 2 small balls of Golden Bear Brown
Sugar Dough for later. Roll the remaining
paste into a sausage, bringing the tail end into a
finer point and leaving the head rounded. Mark
the mouth with the blunt side of a small knife and
push the end of a paintbrush into either side of the
mouth for the dimples. Push the paintbrush handle
into the top of the head for the eye sockets.

2 Make 2 small fins from the reserved paste.
Push a bone tool into the centre of both and
secure to the sides of the body with a little edible
glue. Mark the gills just in front of the fins with a
Dresden tool and the nostrils just above the mouth.

3 Brush a little edible glue in the eye sockets
and push 2 tiny balls of White Sugar Dough
into them, then mark with a Black Food Colour Pen.

4 Stipple all over the eel's body and under the
mouth using a Dresden tool, marking the
paste less as you work towards the tail end.

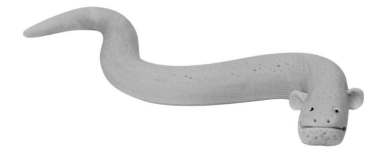

yellow tang fish

edibles

SK Sugar Dough: 3g (pinch) Black,
3g (pinch) Brown, 35g (1¼oz) Yellow

SK Food Colour Pen: Black

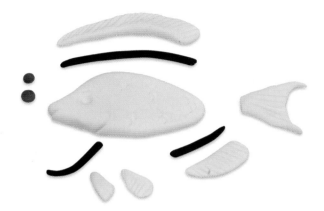

1 Divide the Yellow Sugar Dough as follows: 30g for the body; 3g for the top fin; 1g for the back fin; and 1g divided in half for the lower front fins.

2 Shape a flattened oval for the body. Bring the mouth to a rounded point and make an incision with a small knife. Push the end of a bone tool into the front on each side to create the eye sockets. Mark the gills on both sides with a Dresden tool and mark again above the eye. Push the end of a drinking straw into the paste at a 45° angle in groups of 3 for the scales.

3 Roll the Black Sugar Dough into a long sausage, brush a little edible glue over the top of the body and lay the black paste over the glued area. Cut to size and keep the trimmings. Brush edible glue just in front of the gills and under the head. Bring the black paste to a point at one end and lay the paste over the glued area. Cut to size, bring the cut end to a point and secure down. Brush a little edible glue at the tail end on the underside and secure the remaining black paste in place.

4 Shape the lower front fins from Yellow Sugar Dough and secure with edible glue just behind the gills. Shape the back fin, mark with a Dresden tool and secure to the underside of the body at the back with edible glue. Arrange the fins slightly to one side. Shape the top fin to fit over the top of the black paste, mark with a Dresden tool and secure in place. Shape the tail, bringing the ends out and curling them round. Mark like the other fins and secure to the end of the fish, holding in place until firmly secured in place. Roll the brown paste into 2 balls for the eyes, brush a little edible glue into each of the eye sockets and attach the eyes. Push a Black Food Colour Pen into each one for the pupils.

orange clownfish

edibles

SK Sugar Dough: 2g (pinch)
Black, 40g (1½oz) Orange, 4g
(just under ¼oz) White

SK Food Colour Pen: Black

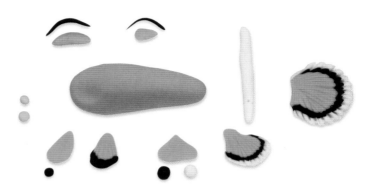

1 Divide the Orange Sugar Dough as follows: 30g for the body; 3g for the tail; 2 pinches for the side fins; 2 pinches for the bottom fins; and 2 small pinches for the top fins.

2 Shape the body and mark the mouth with the blunt side of a small knife. Push a paintbrush into each end of the mouth for dimples and bring the mouth downwards. Slightly flatten the front of the head with your thumb and make the eye sockets with a bone tool.

3 Roll out the White Sugar Dough into a strip 1cm wide. Wrap the white paste around the body at the front, middle and back and cut to size, using edible glue to secure the strips as you go. Reserve the remaining White Sugar Dough to use later.

4 Roll out half the Black Sugar Dough into a long strip and glue on either side of the white strips. Cut to size and secure the ends to the underside of the body.

5 Shape the tail piece from Orange Sugar Dough. Roll out a strip of Black Sugar Dough,

brush a little edible glue around the end of the tail and attach the strip. Repeat with a strip of White Sugar Dough. Mark the tail with a Dresden tool and secure to the body with edible glue.

6 Shape the 2 side fins and repeat the same process as for the tail section. Secure in place on each side of the body. Shape the bottom fins and top fins, attach a strip of black paste (no white), mark both sides with a Dresden tool and secure to the body.

7 Mix together small amounts of Orange and White Sugar Dough for the eyes, divide in half and attach to the eye sockets with edible glue. Push a Black Food Colour Pen into each of the eyes for the pupils.

blue tropical fish

edibles

SK Sugar Dough: 35g (1¼oz) Blue,
3g (pinch) Red

SK Food Colour Pen: Black

1 Divide the Blue Sugar Dough as follows: 25g for the body; 2g for the top fin; 2g for the bottom fin; 2g for the tail; 2 x 1g for the front side fins; and 2 x 1g for the lower front fins.

2 Shape the body of the fish. Make an incision using a small, sharp knife for the mouth and round off the edges. Indent each side of the head using a bone tool for the eye sockets and mark the gills using a Dresden tool. Using a drinking straw at a 45° angle, mark fish scales on the body in groups of 3.

3 Shape the bottom fin, mark with a Dresden tool and secure to the underside of the body with a little edible glue, bringing the fin to one side of the fish for balance.

4 Shape the tail piece, mark both sides using a Dresden tool and secure to the back of the body.

5 Shape the top fin to fit the top of the body and mark with a Dresden tool, gently dragging the paste outwards at the front of the fin. Secure in place with edible glue.

6 Shape the front side fins, mark as before and secure to the body just behind the gills. Shape the lower front fins, mark the tops and attach to the body just under the gill markings with edible glue.

7 Roll 2 small balls of Red Sugar Dough, brush a small amount of edible glue in each eye socket and attach the eyes. Push a Black Food Colour Pen into each eye for the pupils.

sea life cookies

If you're modelling your favourite sea creatures from sugar, why not make some cookies to go with them? These cookies are easy to make and great fun to decorate, too.

edibles

Cookie dough (see page 7)

500g packet SK Instant Mix Royal Icing

SK Professional Liquid Food Colours:
Blackberry, Bluebell, Daffodil, Nasturtium, Poinsettia

equipment

Fish cookie cutter and 6.5cm (2½") round cutter

Templates (see page 12)

Piping nozzle: no. 2

Greaseproof paper piping bags

Small bowls

Scissors

1 Roll out the cookie dough to a thickness of 5mm (¼") and cut out an assortment of shapes using the templates and cutter. Bake as per the recipe (see page 7) and allow to cool before decorating.

2 Make up the Instant Mix Royal Icing following the instructions on the packet. Place into a piping bag with a no. 2 nozzle and pipe an outline around the differently shaped cookies.

3 Add a little cold water to some of the icing to make it slightly runnier then divide this into smaller bowls. Make different colours for each cookie design by mixing a few drops of colouring into each bowl.

4 Place the different coloured icing into greaseproof paper piping bags (with no nozzle), cut off the tip of each bag and carefully flood the icing onto the biscuit within the piped outline. Leave to dry for a couple of hours.

5 Place the coloured royal icing in a piping bag with a no. 2 piping nozzle and pipe details on the cookies. Allow to dry.

WILD

Create your very own safari scene by modelling your own wild animals in sugar.
You can display them on a cake, give them as gifts, or eat them yourself!

snakes

edibles

SK Sugar Dough: 2g (pinch) Black,
14g (½oz) Green, 14g (½oz) Red,
14g (½oz) Yellow

SK Food Colour Pen: Black

1 Reserve 2 small balls of paste from each of the colours for the eyes, then divide each of the colours in half. Alternate the colours, using 2 for each snake.

2 Roll out each piece of paste into a sausage, bring 1 end to a point and flatten slightly at the other end for the head. Lay 1 colour on top of the other then twist and roll the pastes together from the back of the head to the tail. Repeat to make 3 snakes.

3 Brush a little edible glue on the top of the head, roll the reserved balls of paste for the eyes

and attach in place. Push the end of a Black Food Colour Pen into each one.

4 Divide the pinch of Black Sugar Dough into 3, roll into thin sausages and cut an incision in one end. Separate the 2 halves to make a forked tongue. Brush a small amount of edible glue between the 2 colours on the head and gently push the tongue in place. Cut the tongue down to size if it is too long.

5 Twist and curl the snakes into any shape while the paste is still soft.

elephant

edibles

SK Sugar Dough: 2g (pinch) Black, 165g
(5¾oz) White

Important note: Remember to remove the
spaghetti before the model is eaten.

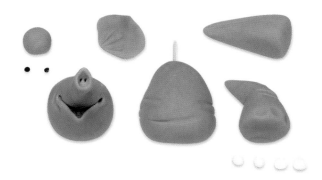

1 Reserve 2 small balls of Black Sugar Dough for
the eyes and 2g of White Sugar Dough for the
toes. Mix together the remaining black and white
paste to make a light grey colour and divide as
follows: 65g for the body; 40g for the head; 4 x 10g
for the legs; 6g for the ears; and a pinch for the tail.

2 Roll out a thin sausage for the tail. Shape the
body of the elephant into a ball and mark
creases on the body and neck with a Dresden tool.
Shape each of the legs into a cone, mark the knees
with a Dresden tool and attach in place with edible
glue. Bring the 2 front legs together. Make 4 indents
in each of the feet with a bone tool and attach 4
white balls for the toes on each foot.

3 Roll the head into a ball and carefully ease the
paste out on one side to form a trunk. Mark
under the trunk with the blunt edge of a small knife,
then use a Dresden tool to make a mouth. Smooth
around the mouth then make large dimples using a
paintbrush.

4 Mark the trunk with a Dresden tool then push a
bone tool into the end. Mark the nostrils with the

Dresden tool. Make 2 small hollows for the eyes
with the bone tool.

5 Push a 7.5cm (3") piece of spaghetti down
into the body, brush a little edible glue around
the neck and ease the head at an angle over the
spaghetti. Make 2 ears and secure in place with
edible glue. Smooth over the join and bend the
ears over slightly.

6 Add 2 small balls of black
paste for the eyes and
mark the eyebrows with a
Black Food Colour Pen.

monkey

edibles

SK Sugar Dough: 77g (2¾oz) Brown, 7g (¼oz) Golden Bear Brown, 1g (small pinch) White, 5g (just under ¼oz) Yellow

Important note: Remember to remove the spaghetti before the model is eaten.

1 Divide the Brown Sugar Dough as follows: 25g for the body; 13g for the head; 8g for the tail; 1g for the ears and nose; 2 x 10g for the hind legs; and 2 x 5g for the arms.

2 Roll a sausage for the tail and bend slightly. Shape the body into a pear shape and secure over the end of the tail with a little edible glue. Shape 3g of Golden Bear Brown Sugar Dough into a flat oval, secure this to the front of the monkey's body and mark halfway down on either side with a Dresden tool.

3 Roll 2 sausages for the legs, make a point at one end and shape the other end into a foot. Mark at the knee with a Dresden tool and bend the leg slightly. Attach to each side of the body with a little edible glue and arrange the legs as required.

4 Shape each of the arms in the same way as for the legs but simply flatten at one end to make the hands. Attach to the top of the body, resting the arms backwards. Push a 7cm (2¾") length of dried spaghetti into the top of the body to help support the head.

5 Shape the head into an oval and secure over the spaghetti at the neck with edible glue. Roll the remaining Golden Bear Brown Sugar Dough into a ball, flatten on one side and secure to the monkey's head for the snout. Gently flatten the top area to support the nose. Push the end of a paintbrush into the paste and pull down slightly to make the mouth.

6 Mark 2 eyebrows on the head with a bone tool, lifting the paste upwards. Divide the White Sugar Dough into 2 balls and attach above the Golden Bear Brown paste with edible glue. Push the end of a Black Food Colour Pen into each of the eyes and mark eyebrows over the raised paste.

7 Pinch out a small ball of the Brown Sugar Dough for a nose, roll into an oval and secure to the front of the snout. Divide the remaining brown paste into 2 for the ears, roll each one into a ball and push the bone tool into each ball on 1 side. Secure to the sides of the head with edible glue.

8 To make the banana divide the Yellow Sugar Dough in half. Shape the first half into a sausage and bring each end to a rounded point to make the banana shape. Divide the other half into 4 parts. To form the banana skin roll each piece into a sausage, flatten and mark with a Dresden tool. Bring all 4 pieces together and pinch at the base, open up the pieces from the top and bend a couple of pieces backwards. Arrange the banana and skin around the monkey.

giraffe

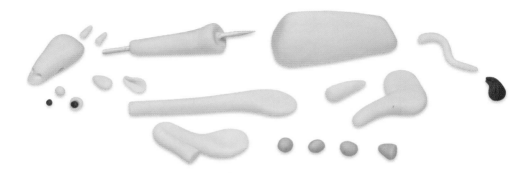

edibles

SK Sugar Dough: 2g (small pinch) Brown, 4g
(just under ¼oz) Golden Bear Brown, 140g
(5oz) Yellow

SK Food Colour Pens: Black, Brown

Cooled, boiled water

Important note: Remember to remove the
wooden skewer before the model is eaten.

1 Divide the Yellow Sugar Dough as follows:
75g for the body; 10g for the neck; 10g for the
head; 4 x 10g for the legs; 1g (small pinch) for the
horns; and 1g (small pinch) for the ears.

2 Shape the body into an oval and pinch a ridge
down the spine. Mark where the leg will be and
at the back of the body with a Dresden tool. Slightly
flatten the chest at the front of the body.

3 Make the 2 back legs, cut 1 short and secure
it under the body. Take the other leg and,
using a little extra paste from the other back leg,
make a thigh at the top. Reserve the remaining
paste for the tail. Mark the leg with a Dresden tool
and secure to the side of the body with edible
glue, bringing the top leg alongside the other one.
Smooth over the joins with a Dresden tool.

4 Make the 2 front legs into sausage shapes,
leaving the top end wider. Bend into shape
and secure to the front of the body, smoothing over
any joins with a Dresden tool.

5 Divide the Golden Bear Brown Sugar Dough
into 4 for the hooves. Roll each piece into a

ball, pinch 2 down to a point for the back hooves and secure to the ends of the legs. Push a bone tool into the centre of the other 2 and secure to the front legs. Tuck them underneath the body.

6 Make a tail from the reserved yellow paste, join this to the back of the body and secure over the hind leg with edible glue.

7 Roll the neck into a sausage shape and push a 12.5cm (5") long wooden barbeque skewer through the middle. Brush a little edible glue over the neck and push the skewer into the body, leaving 2cm exposed for the head. Smooth over the join with a Dresden tool. Leave the neck to dry for a couple of hours before adding the head.

8 Shape the head into a pear and gently shape the long nose between your fingers and thumb. Mark the mouth underneath the nose with the blunt edge of a small knife then use the end of a paintbrush to make dimples and nostrils. Brush edible glue over the neck and ease the head into place over the skewer. Smooth over the join with a Dresden tool.

9 Shape the ears into pear shapes, flatten and wrap around the end of a Dresden tool. Secure to the head with edible glue. Roll the paste for the horns into a sausage, cut in half and attach the cut edges to the top of the head with edible glue.

10 Roll 2 small balls of yellow paste for the eyes, attach to the head and add 2 smaller brown balls on top. Push the end of a Black Food Colour Pen into each one.

11 Use the remaining brown paste to make the end of the tail, mark with a Dresden tool and secure in place with a little edible glue.

12 Use the Brown Food Colour Pen to draw on the giraffe's markings. Make smaller marks around the knees, leaving the ends of the legs clear. Make small marks at the back of the head and draw inside the ears and over the top of the head. Draw inside each nostril, on the dimples and at the end of the nose. Using cooled, boiled water and a paintbrush, brush over the markings to merge the colour over the yellow. Repeat at the end of the tail.

zebra

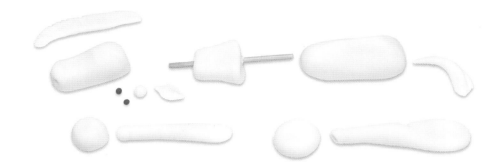

edibles

SK Sugar Dough: 1g (small pinch) Brown, 115g (4¼oz) White

SK Food Colour Pens: Black, Brown

Cooled, boiled water

Important note: Remember to remove the wooden skewer before the model is eaten.

1 Divide the White Sugar Dough as follows: 45g for the body; 10g for the head; 10g for the neck; 6g for the mane; 2 x 8g for the front legs and 2 x 10g for the back legs; 5g for the tail; and 2g for the ears.

2 Shape the body into an oval and pinch a ridge down the back for the spine. Shape the front legs and mark with a Dresden tool at the hooves and knees. Attach to the front of the body with edible glue and cross over the legs at the ankles. Smooth over any joins using a Dresden tool.

3 Shape the back legs and mark the hooves and knee joints as before with a Dresden tool. Secure to the back of the body, bringing the legs towards the front. Push a bone tool into the underside of each hoof.

4 Make a tail section and mark the hair with a Dresden tool, dragging the paste downwards to make it uneven. Secure to the back of the zebra with edible glue.

5 Shape the neck and pinch along the back edge for the spine. Carefully push a 7.5cm (3") long wooden barbeque skewer through the neck. Brush a little edible glue over the top of the body at the neck area and push the skewer down through the body. Smooth over the join with a Dresden tool. Leave the neck to dry for a couple of hours before attempting to put the head in place.

6 Shape the head into a sausage shape and cut open a mouth with a small, sharp knife. Shape and mark the mouth and teeth with a Dresden tool. Push the end of a paintbrush into the paste above the mouth for the nostrils. Push a bone tool into the paste nearer the back of the head for the eye sockets. Secure the head carefully over the skewer with edible glue and smooth over any joins.

7 Make a long strip of white paste for the mane and mark all the way down on both sides with a Dresden tool. Cut a couple of sections out with a sharp knife along the top edge and secure to the back of the head and neck with edible glue so that the mane comes to just above the eyes.

8 Make 2 ears, gently bend them around a Dresden tool then pinch the top of each ear. Attach to the head on either side of the mane with edible glue.

9 Roll small balls of Brown Sugar Dough and attach inside the eye sockets with edible glue. Push the end of a Black Food Colour Pen into each eye for the pupils.

10 Draw over the hooves with a Brown Food Colour Pen then brush over each one with a small amount of cooled, boiled water to dilute the colour. Mark the tail and inside the ears with the Black Food Colour Pen and wash over again with cooled, boiled water, leaving it lighter towards the end of the tail. Draw lines over the zebra with the black pen, making thicker markings around the hooves, nose, mouth and the ends of the mane.

lion

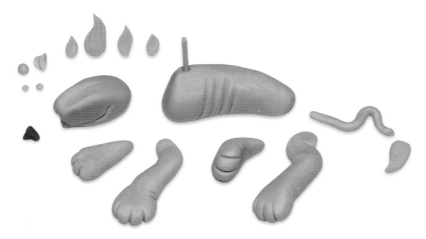

edibles

SK Sugar Dough: 2g (pinch) Brown, 210g (7½oz) Golden Bear Brown, 70g (2½oz) Orange

SK Food Colour Pen: Black

Important note: Remember to remove the wooden skewer before the model is eaten.

1 Divide the Golden Bear Brown Sugar Dough as follows: 85g for the body; 13g for the front paw and 25g for the front leg; 13g for the back paw and 25g for the back leg; 5g for the tail; 38g for the head; and 2g for the ears.

2 Shape the body into a sausage, making it slightly wider towards the front. Mark the ribs with a Dresden tool.

3 Model the front and back paws into pear shapes, flatten the wide end slightly and mark 3 times with the blunt edge of a small knife. Make creases around the ankles with a Dresden tool. Cut the pointed end of the pear shape at an angle and secure to the body with edible glue.

4 Roll sausage shapes for the front and back legs, flatten slightly and mark the paws and ankles as before. Secure to the body and smooth the joins. Rest the back paws over each other.

5 Roll the tail into a sausage and secure to the back of the body. Model a teardrop from 4g of

Orange Sugar Dough for the end of the tail, mark with a Dresden tool and secure to the tail.

6 Take 5g of Golden Bear Brown Sugar Dough from the paste for the head, shape into a wedge and attach to the top of the body where the head will sit with edible glue. Smooth over the join. Start to build up the mane with small sections of paste around the wedge and over the body and front limbs. Make small teardrop shapes from Orange Sugar Dough, mark with a Dresden tool, pinch the paste to a point and secure at the wide end. Build up a couple of layers of hair, twisting and turning them in different directions.

7 Shape the remaining paste for the head into an oval, pinch to a point for a chin and flatten the nose area. Run your finger down the front of the head from the top to flatten it a little. Use a small knife to mark the mouth at the front and along both sides of the head. Push a 6.5cm (2½") long wooden barbeque skewer into the neck, brush a little edible glue over the paste and ease the head over the skewer. Continue to build up the mane in small sections around the back and the sides of the head.

8 Make 2 indents with a bone tool for the eyes and run a Dresden tool down from the top of the head to the level of the eyes. Make flattened pear shapes for the ears, wrap around the end of a Dresden tool and secure to the top of the head with edible glue. Finish adding the hair for the mane, this time from the front of the head working towards the back, leaving a couple of tufts upright at the top of the head to fill any gaps.

9 Draw around the eye sockets with a Black Food Colour Pen. Make 2 small balls of Golden Bear Brown paste for the eyes, secure into the sockets and push the end of the food pen into each of the eyes for pupils.

10 Mark the whiskers on the face with a Dresden tool. For the nose, shape the pinch of Brown Sugar Dough into a triangle, mark down the centre with a blunt edge of a knife and secure in place. Push the end of a paintbrush into either side of the central line for the nostrils.

11 Using the Black Food Colour Pen, draw the claws on all the paws and a pad underneath the paw resting upwards.

wild animal cupcakes

These wild cupcakes are decorated with quick and simple designs, such as paw prints, to complement the sugar models. Before you start this project, make sure you have all the basic items needed for covering a cake (see page 8) plus the extra edibles and equipment listed here.

edibles

Decoration quantities are based on 28 mini cupcakes and 42 cupcakes baked in animal print large and mini cases (see recipe on pages 6 to 7)

Jam filling

Sugarpaste: 1.5kg (3lb 5oz) white

SK Sugar Dough: 205g (7¼oz) Black, 105g (3¾oz) Brown, 145g (5¼oz) Golden Bear Brown, 55g (2oz) Green, 120g (4¼oz) Orange, 55g (2oz) Red, 255g (9oz) White, 175g (6¼oz) Yellow

SK Food Colour Pen: Black

equipment

2.5cm and 6.5cm (1" and 2½") round cutters

Paintbrush: no. 2

Paw print templates (see page 26)

mini cupcake designs

1 Level the top of each mini cupcake with a knife and spread a small amount of jam on the top. Roll out 500g of white sugarpaste and cut rounds with a 2.5cm cutter. Place onto the mini cupcakes and smooth over with a smoother to seal the cake and create a neat finish.

2 Knead a little white vegetable fat into 200g of Black Sugar Dough and roll out. Cut out an equal amount from the 4 paw print designs using the templates and secure to the top of each mini cupcake with edible glue.

cupcake designs

3 Level the tops of the cupcakes and spread a little jam on each, as above. Roll out the remaining white sugarpaste and cut out rounds with a 6.5cm cutter. Smooth each cupcake over with a smoother to seal the cake and create a neat finish. Divide the cupcakes into equal groups

for the designs you wish to make: choose from elephant, monkey, lion, giraffe, snake, banana and bone.

4 Elephant: knead together a small ball of Black Sugar Dough into 250g of White Sugar Dough to make a grey mix. Divide into 6 equal amounts and follow the instructions for the elephant's head on page 29.

5 Monkey: divide 90g of Brown, 25g of Golden Bear Brown and 6g of White Sugar Dough each into 6 equal amounts and make 6 heads following the instructions on page 31.

6 Lion: divide 120g of Orange and 90g of Golden Bear Brown Sugar Dough each into 6 equal amounts. Pinch 6 small balls from Brown Sugar Dough for the noses and follow the instructions on page 37 for making the lion's head.

7 Giraffe: divide 90g of Yellow and 12g of Brown Sugar Dough each into 6 equal amounts and follow the instructions for making the giraffe's head on page 33.

8 Snake: make a snake using 7g of Sugar Dough in 2 colours, following the instructions on page 28.

9 Bananas: divide 30g of Yellow Sugar Dough into 6 and follow the instructions on page 31 for making the bananas.

10 Bones: divide 30g of Golden Bear Brown Sugar Dough into 6. Roll each piece of paste into a sausage, making it slightly fatter at each end. Mark down the centre of each end with a Dresden tool then twist the bone gently.

11 Attach all the heads, bananas and bones to the tops of the cupcakes using edible glue.

PETS

We all love our pets so what better subject for a special celebration cake?
This collection of our favourite furry friends is perfect for animal lovers everywhere.

guinea pig

edibles

SK Sugar Dough: 50g (1¾oz)
Black, 10g (just under ½oz)
Golden Bear Brown, 2g (pinch)
Red, 11g (just under ½oz)
White

1 Mix 2g of White Sugar Dough with a tiny amount of Red to make pale pink. Reserve a small amount for the nose then divide the remaining paste into 4. Shape each piece into a pear shape, flatten the wide end, make 3 incisions with a small knife for the toes and spread them out.

2 Shape 40g of Black Sugar Dough into a sausage for the body and mark all over with a Dresden tool. Push a small piece of dried spaghetti into one end at an angle. Secure over the feet with a little edible glue. Add 2g of White Sugar Dough to the left front of the body and texture with a Dresden tool to resemble hair. Add 3g of Golden Bear Brown to the right side of the body and texture as before.

3 Shape the head from the remaining White Sugar Dough. Add 5g of Golden Bear Brown Sugar Dough to either side and smooth in. Attach the head to the body over the spaghetti then drag the hair back to the neck area.

4 Indent the eye sockets with a bone tool. Roll 2 small balls of Black Sugar Dough, brush a little edible glue in each socket and push the eyes

in place. Mark each eye with the Dresden tool and add the tiniest piece of white for a highlight.

5 Shape a triangle for the nose from the reserved pink paste and attach with edible glue. Mark 2 nostrils with the end of a paintbrush and a central line from the base with a Dresden tool.

6 To make the ears, split a pinch of Golden Bear Brown Sugar Dough in half, roll each piece into a ball and flatten. Pinch at the edge and secure to the head. Add long lengths of black hair to the back of the guinea pig by rolling small sections to a fine point and securing to the back in a random pattern.

dog

edibles

SK Sugar Dough: 2g (pinch) Brown,
75g (2½oz) Golden Bear Brown, 1g
(small pinch) Red, 2g (pinch) White

SK Food Colour Pen: Black

1 Divide the Golden Bear Brown Sugar Dough as follows: 25g for the body; 4 x 7g for the legs; 15g for the head; 1g (small pinch) for the tail; and 2 x 1g for the ears.

2 Roll the body into a smooth pear shape. Roll 4 pear shapes for the legs and mark twice at the wide end with the blunt edge of a small knife for the toes. Position the 2 back legs together at the points with the toes pointing outward and secure the body over the top. Attach the 2 front legs in place.

3 Pinch a ball of Red Sugar Dough between your finger and thumb to form a disc. Attach to the top of the body and front legs with a little edible glue.

4 Roll the tail into a long pear shape, bend over and secure to the back of the dog with edible glue.

5 Shape the head into a rounded pear and gently flatten the top with your finger. Push a drinking straw into the larger end at a 45° angle and make dimples with a piece of dried spaghetti. Secure the head over the red disc with edible glue.

6 Flatten 2 tiny balls of White Sugar Dough and attach to the flat part of the head. Mark the pupils and eyebrows with a Black Food Colour Pen. Divide the Brown Sugar Dough in half, roll 1 piece into an oval and secure to the front of the head for a nose. Roll the remaining Brown Sugar Dough into small balls and push into the body of the dog to create spots.

7 Shape the ears, flatten slightly and attach to the top of the head, resting them backwards as if they are blowing in the wind.

cat and mice

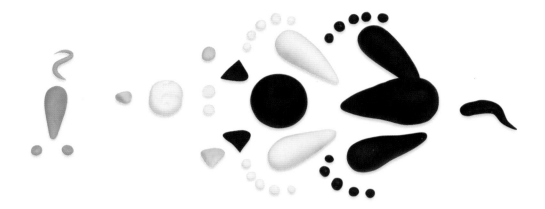

edibles

cat

SK Sugar Dough: 50g (1¾oz) Black, 1g (small pinch) Red, 20g (¾oz) White

SK Food Colour Pen: Black

mice

SK Sugar Dough: 1g (small pinch) Black, 5g (just under ¼oz) White

SK Food Colour Pen: Black

equipment

Food-grade foam sponge

cat

1 Divide the Black Sugar Dough as follows: 20g for the body; 2 x 7g for the back legs; 10g for the head; 1g for the tail; and 1g divided in half for the ears. Divide the White Sugar Dough as follows: 2 x 7g for the front legs; 2g for the muzzle; 1g for the ears and nose; and 2 tiny balls for the eyes.

2 Shape the body into a pear shape. Roll 5 small balls for the toes from the paste for each of the back legs, then shape the legs into pear shapes as well. Roll the head into a ball and gently squeeze it between your finger and thumb to flatten it slightly. Make the front legs and toes as per the back legs but using White Sugar Dough.

3 Roll a ball for the muzzle, then flatten between your finger and thumb. Mark down the centre from the top with the blunt edge of a small knife then push a drinking straw into the paste at a 45° angle on either side of the line. Push a piece of dried spaghetti into the paste at each end for dimples.

4 To assemble the cat, put the 2 back legs point-to-point, position the body of the cat over the legs and secure with a little edible glue. Brush some edible glue around the end of each leg and attach the toes. Secure the 2 front legs to either side of the front of the body, along with the toes as before. Attach the head to the neck area with edible glue, resting on the front legs. Brush a little edible glue on the front of the head and secure the muzzle.

5 Roll 2 small white balls, flatten them and attach above the muzzle for the eyes. Push a Black Food Colour Pen into the centre of each eye for the pupils.

6 Roll the tail into a sausage, bring one end to a point, cut the other end at an angle and secure to the back end of the cat. Bend the tail slightly and support until dry if necessary with a piece of food-grade foam sponge.

7 Mix a small amount of Red Sugar Dough into the White to make a light pink colour for the nose and inner ears. Roll a small ball for the nose, shape into a pyramid and secure to the top of the muzzle with edible glue, keeping the flat side at the top of the nose. Divide the remaining pink paste in half and shape into 2 flattened triangles. Repeat with the remaining black paste. Rest each pink triangle on top of the black, press them together and cut down to size. Bend each ear around the end of a Dresden tool and secure to the top of the cat's head with edible glue.

mice

1 Mix together the Black and White Sugar Dough to make a light grey colour and divide into 3 balls. Make a mouse from each ball: pinch out 2 small balls for the ears and another for the tail. Shape the rest of the paste into a pear shape and bring the top end to a point for the nose.

2 Roll the tail into a long, thin sausage that is pointed at one end. Secure the body on top of the tail with edible glue.

3 Roll 2 balls for the ears and push the end of a bone tool into one side of the ball. Attach to the top end of the body around 5mm from the tip of the nose. Mark the eyes on the mouse using a Black Food Colour Pen.

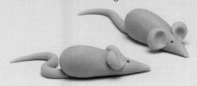

rabbit

edibles

SK Sugar Dough: 2g (pinch) Black, 12g (just under ½oz) Golden Bear Brown, 1g (small pinch) Green, 4g (just under ¼oz) Orange, 35g (1¼oz) White

1 Divide the White Sugar Dough as follows: 10g for the body; 9g for the head; 2 x 1g for the front legs; 2 x 5g for the back legs; and 2g for the tail. Divide the Golden Bear Brown Sugar Dough as follows: 9g for the body; 2g for the ears; and use the remaining paste for the eye patch and spots.

2 Bring the 2 colours together for the body and shape into an oval. Shape the 2 front legs and mark the toes twice with a Dresden tool. Secure the body on top of the legs with edible glue. Shape both the back legs, flatten at the thigh slightly, mark the toes and base of the thigh with a Dresden tool and secure to either side of the body.

3 Shape the tail into a pear and mark with a Dresden tool. Attach to the back of the body with edible glue.

4 Push a 3cm (1¹⁄₈") long piece of dried spaghetti into the body to help support the head. Pinch out a small piece of paste from the head for the teeth and reserve. Shape the remainder of the paste into an oval, mark the mouth with the blunt edge of a small knife in an upside down 'Y' shape and stipple the whisker area with the end of a Dresden tool. Make a set of teeth from the reserved paste, mark down the centre with the blunt side of a small knife and secure to the underside of the mouth with a little edible glue. Brush a little edible glue around the base of the neck, ease the head over the dried spaghetti and secure in place.

5 Roll small balls from the Golden Bear Brown Sugar Dough and push into the sides of the body and back legs. Push another ball of paste over the eye area to make a patch and push the end of a bone tool into the head twice to create the eye sockets.

6 Shape a triangle of Golden Bear Brown Sugar Dough for the nose and attach to the front of the head above the markings for the mouth. Model

each of the ears into long pear shapes, flatten slightly and attach to the top of the rabbit's head. Roll 2 small balls from the Black Sugar Dough, brush a little edible glue into the eye sockets and push the black paste into place. Mark both eyes with the end of a Dresden tool. Take the tiniest piece of white paste and push it into the black eyes for highlights.

7 Divide the Orange Sugar Dough in half and shape into carrots. Push the end of a paintbrush into the top of each one and mark down each carrot randomly with a knife. Divide the Green Sugar Dough in half, roll each piece into a ball then push the end of a paintbrush into the centre of each one, bringing the paste to a point between your fingers. Take a pair of small scissors, cut 5 incisions for the carrot tops, soften the edges between your fingers and bend each one out. Secure inside the hole at the top of each carrot using a little edible glue.

shetland pony

edibles

SK Sugar Dough: 60g (2oz) Black, 110g (4oz) Brown, 2g (pinch) Golden Bear Brown

1 Divide the Brown Sugar Dough as follows: 50g for the body; 35g for the head; 2 x 6g for the back legs; 2 x 4g for the front legs; and 1g for the ears.

2 Shape the body into a pear shape and sit it on the wide end. Push a 7cm (2¾") long piece of dried spaghetti down through the neck to give the head maximum support. Shape the back legs, flatten slightly at the thigh end and mark with a Dresden tool. Attach to both sides of the body with edible glue.

3 Roll out the front legs, mark with a Dresden tool and cut the top of the legs at an angle. Secure to the front of the body at the cut end and rest them in front of the body.

4 Make 4 hooves from the Golden Bear Brown Sugar Dough, shape 2 into small balls and push the end of a bone tool into the underside to make the hoof shape. Attach these to the back legs. Pinch the 2 remaining balls on one side and secure to the underside of the front legs with edible glue. Shape the head, mark a mouth with the blunt edge of a small knife and push the end of a paintbrush into each end of the mouth to make large dimples. Push the paintbrush into the paste above the mouth for the nostrils and mark above them with a Dresden tool.

5 Brush a little edible glue around the base of the exposed spaghetti and ease the head into position. Divide the remaining brown paste in half for the ears, shape into flattened pear shapes, curl around a Dresden tool and secure to the top of the horse's head.

6 Shape 10g of Black Sugar Dough into a long pear shape for the tail and mark with a Dresden tool, dragging the paste down at the ends to look like hair. Secure to the back of the horse's body with edible glue. Push the Dresden tool into where the tail joins the body and bend the tail around.

7 Build up the mane in small sections at a time, shaping small balls from the remaining Black Sugar Dough into teardrops and marking with a Dresden tool to resemble hair. Attach to the back of the head, starting at the base of the neck and working up to the back of the ears. Continue to add hair over the front of the pony's eyes, working back towards the ears to create a top parting. Secure a final piece of hair on the top to fill any gaps.

pet party cake

If you're planning a party, what better way to celebrate than with a cake covered with modelled pets? Before you start this project, make sure you have all the basic items needed for covering a cake (see page 8) plus the extra edibles and equipment listed here.

edibles

15cm and 20.5cm (6" and 8") round sponge cakes
675g (1lb 7¾oz) buttercream
Jam filling (optional)
Sugarpaste: 2kg (4lb 6½oz) green
SK Sugar Dough: 2g (pinch) Blue, 2g (pinch) Golden Bear Brown, 8g (¼oz) Red, 25g (1oz) White
SK Food Colour Pen: Black
Small amount of royal icing
Cooled, boiled water

equipment

30.5cm (12") cake drum
2.25m (89") x 15mm wide ribbon: pale yellow
Paintbrush: no. 2
Scissors
3 dowelling rods
Sugar shaper
Non-toxic glue stick

covering the cakes and drum

1 Fill the cakes with buttercream (and jam) and place the base cake onto the cake drum. Cover the cake with a layer of buttercream to help the sugarpaste stick.

2 Roll out 1.25kg of green sugarpaste on a non-stick board, cover the whole cake and smooth over the top and sides with a smoother. Cut away any excess paste from the base of the cake with a small, sharp knife and reserve the trimmings.

3 Push 3 dowelling rods into the base cake for support. Mark the dowels with a Black Food Colour Pen level with the sugarpaste covering and remove from the cake. Place the dowels side-by-side on the work surface and score with a knife at the highest mark (so that they are all the same length). Snap the dowels to size and push back into the cake.

4 Cover the smaller cake in the same way as before, smooth, trim around the base and reserve the sugarpaste trimmings. Spoon a small

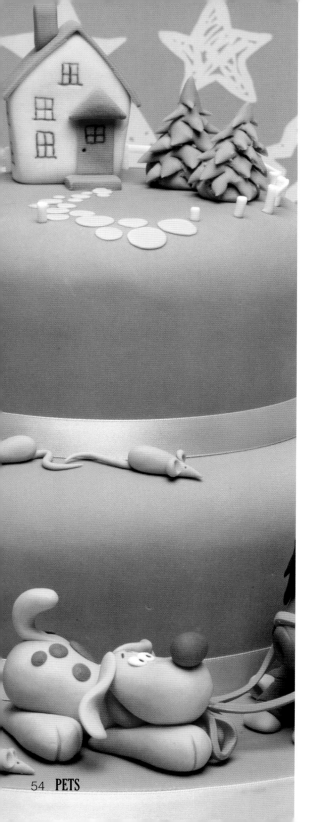

amount of royal icing over each of the dowels and position the top cake centrally on the base cake. Smooth over the sugarpaste covering again.

5 Knead the remaining green sugarpaste, roll out into a strip long enough to go around the base cake and cut a straight edge along one side. Dampen the exposed cake drum with a little cooled, boiled water and attach the strip around the base of the cake with the cut edge against the cake. Cut to size and smooth over the join with a smoother.

6 Cut a length of ribbon for the base of each cake and secure in place by brushing a little royal icing on the ends of the ribbon. Attach ribbon to the edge of the cake drum using a non-toxic glue stick, being careful not to come into contact with the sugarpaste. Cut to size and secure the end down.

trees

7 Divide 75g of green sugarpaste into 6 equal parts. Shape each piece into a cone and push the end of a Dresden tool into the base of the cone for support. Using a pair of scissors, make small incisions and lift upwards, starting at the top and working downwards. Work all around the cone to form a tree. Carefully slip the tree off the Dresden tool and leave to dry. Repeat to make 6 trees altogether. Secure to the top of the cake and cake drum when firm using edible glue.

house

8 Knead together 15g of White Sugar Dough with a pinch of Blue to make a pale blue colour.

Shape into a house and set aside. Roll out the Red Sugar Dough and cut a 2cm x 1cm rectangle for the door and a 2cm x 8cm rectangle for the roof. Brush edible glue over the top of the house shape and attach the roof. Knead the red trimmings together again, roll out thickly and cut a 1cm x 2cm doorstep and a 2cm x 1.5cm x 1.5cm triangle for the porch. Secure the house to the top of the cake with edible glue, then attach the door, porch and doorstep in place. Knead together the trimmings and make a small ball for the chimneypot and a squared off rectangular shape with the end cut off at an angle for the chimney. Secure to the top of the house with edible glue. Draw windows onto the front door and on all 4 sides of the house with a Black Food Colour Pen.

fencing

9 Knead a little white vegetable fat in to 10g of White Sugar Dough and fill the barrel of a sugar shaper fitted with the medium hole disc. Push the paste through to create a length approximately 20cm long and cut into 1cm pieces for the posts. Change the disc to the smallest slit disc and push through more white paste to make a piece 30.5cm long. Cut into fence panels 2cm long and set aside to dry. When dry, secure the upright posts to the top of the cake with edible glue and the fence panels on the outside alternately at the top and bottom of the posts.

pathway

10 Knead 2g of Golden Bear Brown Sugar Dough with white vegetable fat, pinch out small amounts at a time, roll into balls and press into the sugarpaste on the top of the cake. Start from the step at the front door with tiny balls, getting bigger towards the edge of the cake.

pets

11 Attach your favourite modelled pets to the cake drum around the cake using edible glue.

DINOSAURS

Bring the prehistoric world back to life by modelling dinosaurs for your special occasion. Make them scary with sharp teeth and pointed claws, or turn them into friendly dinosaurs with bright colours and a big smile!

t. rex

edibles

SK Sugar Dough: 35g (1¼oz) Brown, 180g (6¼oz) Green, 3g (pinch) White

SK Food Colour Pen: Black

Important note: Remember to remove the wooden skewer before the model is eaten.

1 Reserve 2g of the Brown Sugar Dough for the claws. Knead together the Green and remaining Brown Sugar Dough to make a khaki colour and divide the paste as follows: 170g for the body, head and tail; 2 x 15g for the hind legs; 2 x 1g for the arms; 2g for the top of the head; and 2g for the eye sockets.

2 Roll the body into a fat sausage, ease out the paste to create a tail, then bring it to a point and bend upwards. To shape the head at the other end, ease out the paste to create a long neck, bend over the top and take off a ball for the head. Push a 10cm (4") long wooden barbeque skewer into the body from the base to support the head, then ease the head onto the skewer. Gently pull the paste forward at the front of the head to a rounded point. Make an incision for the mouth and open slightly. Mark the sides of the mouth with a Dresden tool and smooth over the cut edges with your finger.

3 Mark the bridge of the nose at the top of the head with a Dresden tool and make the nostrils with a paintbrush. Brush a little edible glue over the eye area and at the top of the head, shape a wedge of paste for the top of the head, secure in place and mark with a Dresden tool.

4 Roll 2 eyes from White Sugar Dough and attach to the top of the head. Roll 2 small lengths of the khaki paste for the eyelids, secure over the eyeballs and mark with a Dresden tool. Mark the eyes with a Black Food Colour Pen.

5 Define the head by running the Dresden tool down both sides of the neck. Leave the head to dry a little.

6 Shape the hind legs into sausage shapes, making them thinner in the middle. Flatten and round off at 1 end for the thigh, then flatten slightly at the other end and cut 2 incisions for the 3 toes. Smooth the edges and push the end of a bone tool into the end of each toe. Pinch a small amount of paste at the back of the foot to make a 4th toe and mark above the foot and base of the thigh with a Dresden tool. Secure 1 leg to the side of the body with the toes pointing upwards. Bend the top of the other leg at the thigh and secure to the other side with the foot resting flat.

7 Roll each of the front limbs into a sausage, narrow slightly in the middle and mark with a Dresden tool. Cut 1cm down the centre at one end and shape each piece into a point. Round off the other end and attach to the body, bringing one hand over the other.

8 Brush edible glue along the inside of the lower jaw. To make the lower teeth, roll small, pointed sausages from White Sugar Dough and cut to size with a sharp knife. Starting at the back of the mouth attach the smaller teeth with the end of a Dresden tool, working towards bigger teeth at the front. Repeat the same process for the top teeth, which sit in front of the lower teeth.

9 Divide the reserved brown paste into 6 small balls, make small points on each of them and secure to the toes with edible glue.

alligator

edibles

SK Sugar Dough: 5g (just under ¼oz) Black, 165g (5¾oz) Green

SK Food Colour Pen: Black

equipment

Tweezers

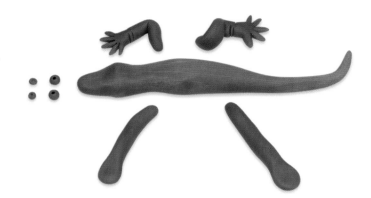

1. Mix the Green and Black Sugar Dough to make dark green and divide as follows: 120g for the body and head; 2 small balls for the eyes; 2 slightly smaller balls for the nostrils; 2 x 10g for front legs; and 2 x 12g for the back legs.

2. Shape the body and head into a long sausage, bring the tail end to a point and flatten the top. Shape the head by easing the paste outwards, then pinch the back of the head and the end of the body. Mark from the back of the head and down the body and tail with tweezers: pinch the paste but don't close the tweezers completely.

3. Mark the mouth and bring it downwards with a Dresden tool. Use the end of a paintbrush to make large dimples.

4. Brush a little edible glue on the nose and attach the nostrils, then push the end of a paintbrush into the centre of both.

5. Mark the eyebrows with a Dresden tool and secure the eyeballs to the top of the head with edible glue. Push a Black Food Colour Pen into the eyes.

6. Bend the body and tail slightly to make the alligator more animated. Shape the front legs into sausage shapes and flatten one end for the foot. Make 4 incisions into the foot with a small knife and spread out the toes. Smooth over the cut edges. Mark the knees and ankles with a Dresden tool, bend each leg at the knee and secure to the body with edible glue. Repeat for the back legs but bend the top of the limb in the opposite direction and point the feet forwards.

diplodocus

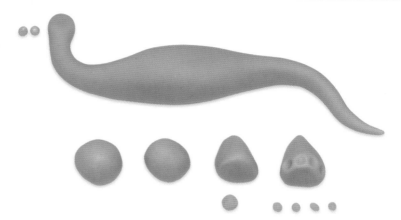

edibles

SK Sugar Dough: 25g (1oz)
Blue, 1g (small pinch) Orange,
90g (3oz) White

SK Food Colour Pen: Black

1 Knead together the Blue and White Sugar Dough to make a pale blue colour. Divide the paste as follows: 85g for the body and head; 2 small balls for the eyes; and 4 x 6g for the legs.

2 Shape the body into a ball, pull out the paste to a point to make a tail then model a slightly fatter head and neck, bending it upwards and bending the head over slightly. Mark the mouth with the blunt edge of a small knife.

3 Shape each of the legs into a cone and attach to the sides of the body with edible glue.

4 Brush a little edible glue on top of the head and attach the eyes. Push the end of a Black Food Colour Pen into each one for the pupils.

5 Mark the toes at the base of each foot with a bone tool and brush a little edible glue into each one. Roll small balls from the orange paste and secure to each foot in the indents.

6 Kink the tail carefully into a natural position.

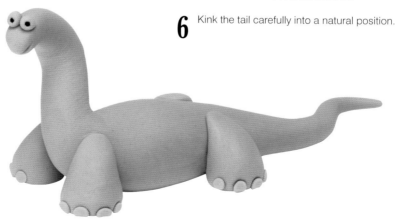

triceratops

edibles

SK Sugar Dough: 165g (5¾oz) Green, 2g (pinch) white

SK Food Colour Pen: Black

equipment

Small piece of food-grade foam sponge

Important note: Remember to remove the wooden skewer before the model is eaten.

1 Divide the Green Sugar Dough as follows: 58g for the body and tail; 2 x 16g for the back legs; 2 x 9g for the front legs; 28g for the head; 5g for the neck; 20g for the back collar; 2g for the back collar spines; and 2g for the 3 horns.

2 Pinch out a small ball of Green Sugar Dough from the paste for the 3 horns, make a small horn for the nose and bend a little. Divide the remaining paste into 2 balls and shape each one into a sausage shape. Roll one end to a point and bend in the middle. Set all 3 horns aside to dry.

3 Shape the body into an oval, ease the paste out for the tail, bring this down to a point and bend upwards. Rest the front of the body on a piece of food-grade foam sponge for support.

4 Roll the 2 back legs into sausage shapes and flatten one end for the foot. Mark the toes with the blunt edge of a small knife and use a Dresden tool to mark the front and back of the knees. Secure to the sides of the body with edible glue. Repeat the same process to make the front legs, mark in the same way and secure to either side of the chest with edible glue.

5 Push a 5cm (2") long wooden barbeque skewer into the front of the body at the neck, leaving 2cm exposed to support the head. Leave to dry for a couple of hours before adding the head and collar to the body.

6 Shape the back collar into a semicircle and make it thinner around the edge. Secure to the top of the body over the wooden skewer using edible glue. Brush a little edible glue on the outside edge of the collar. Roll several small balls of paste for the back collar spines, flatten them, bring each one to a point and secure to the collar. Leave the lower edge clear of points.

7 Make a small wedge for the neck and attach to the body at the lower edge of the collar with edible glue. The thicker end of the wedge should be at the base to help support the head.

8 Shape the head into an oval, tease the paste into a point at one end for the mouth and pinch the paste between your fingers on each side of the head to form small cheeks. Push the end of a paintbrush into the front of the head for the nostrils and again at the top of the head and above the nostrils for the horns to fit in later. Push a bone tool into the head just below the horns for the eye sockets. Use the blunt edge of a small knife to mark a 1cm wide mouth then push the end of a paintbrush into the paste on either side of the mouth for dimples. Mark the edge of each nostril with a Dresden tool.

9 Brush edible glue around the base of the wooden skewer and ease the head over the skewer, securing it to the body. Roll 2 small balls of White Sugar Dough, brush a little edible glue into the eye sockets and push the eyeballs into place. Push the tip of a Black Food Colour Pen into each eyeball and mark 2 small lines on the outside edge of the eyes.

10 Secure the horns in place in each of the holes with a small amount of edible glue.

stegosaurus

edibles

SK Sugar Dough: 150g (5¼oz) Orange, 5g
(just under ¼oz) Red, 5g (just under ¼oz)
White

SK Food Colour Pen: Black

1 Roll out the Red Sugar Dough to a 3mm thickness and cut 14 house shapes in varying sizes for the spines down the dinosaur's back. Set aside to dry.

2 Roll half the White Sugar Dough into a thin sausage. Cut 4 equal lengths for the horns on the tail, round off the ends, bend slightly and leave to dry.

3 Divide the Orange Sugar Dough as follows: 100g for the body, head and tail; 2 x 10g for the front legs; and 2 x 13g for the back legs.

4 Roll a ball for the body, ease out the paste to a point for the tail and bend around, then do the same for the head and neck, making it slightly thicker and bending it upwards. Bring the front of the face to a point and make a mouth opening 1cm wide with a small, sharp knife. Push the end of a paintbrush into each end of the mouth for dimples and gently open the mouth a little.

5 Push the end of a paintbrush into the end of the tail 4 times. Make 14 incisions along the back of the body with a small knife, open them up slightly and brush a little edible glue inside each one. Secure the red spines into the incisions in the back, working from small to large and back to small towards the tail. Brush a little glue into the holes at the tail end and push the 4 white horns into place.

6 Shape each of the legs into an elongated cone, then mark across the front of the foot and behind the knee with a Dresden tool. Bend each leg at the knee and secure to the sides of the body with edible glue. Mark the front of each foot with a bone tool for the toes, roll 16 small balls from the White Sugar Dough, brush a small amount of edible glue into each indent and secure the toes in place.

7 Roll 2 small, white balls for the eyes, brush a little edible glue on the top of the head and attach. Push the tip of a Black Food Colour Pen into each eye for the pupils.

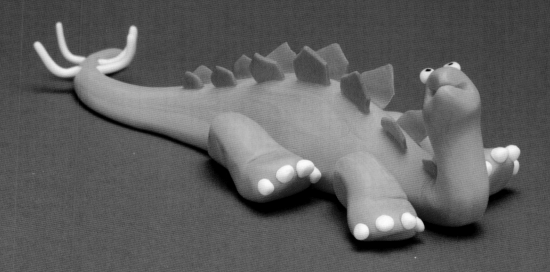

woolly mammoth

edibles

SK Sugar Dough: 305g (10¾oz) Brown, 2g
(pinch) Golden Bear Brown, 8g (¼oz) White

SK Food Colour Pen: Black

equipment

Small piece of food-grade sponge

Important note: Remember to remove the
wooden skewer before the model is eaten.

1 Divide the Brown Sugar Dough as follows: 4 x
20g for the legs; 160g for the body; 30g for the
head; 20g for the trunk; 2g for both ears; and 10g
for the hair on top of the head.

2 To make the tusks divide 6g of White Sugar
Dough in half and roll each piece into a
sausage that is slightly thinner at one end. Bend
each one into a curve and then leave to dry.

3 Shape each of the legs into a short cone
and mark with a Dresden tool very roughly to
resemble thick hair. Push the end of a bone tool into
the each foot 4 times for the toes and brush edible
glue into each indentation. Roll 16 tiny balls of White
Sugar Dough and push the toes into place at the
base of each foot. Position a piece of food-grade
sponge between the 4 legs to help support the
body.

4 Reserve a small ball of paste from the body to
make the tail later. Shape the rest of the paste
into a fat sausage that is larger at one end for the

shoulders, narrow the waist slightly between your finger and thumb and then pinch a ridge across the top of the back for the spine. Mark over the whole body with a Dresden tool for the hair. Brush edible glue over the tops of the 4 legs and secure the body on the top. Drag the Dresden tool down the sides of the body to join it to the legs neatly.

5 Roll out a thin sausage from the reserved paste and secure it to the back of the mammoth for the tail.

6 Shape the head into an oval, flatten the front gently with your finger and push the large end of a bone tool into either side of the head for the tusks to fit in. Attach the head to the top of the shoulders with edible glue. Mark hair around the base of the head with a Dresden tool to hide the join and to help secure the head into place.

7 Roll a sausage shape for the trunk, making it smaller at one end. Run your finger down one side of the trunk to flatten it slightly, mark sections down the trunk with the blunt edge of a small knife and attach to the front of the head with edible glue. Bend the end of the trunk upwards and hollow out the end with a bone tool. Smooth over the join at the front of the face with your finger. Make 2 indentations for the eye sockets with a bone tool.

8 Brush edible glue into the holes made for the tusks, ease each tusk into place and support with the sponge piece from under the body (the legs should be dry enough to support the body

now). Mark the paste around each of the tusks with a Dresden tool to resemble hair.

9 Make 2 pear shapes for the ears, flatten and wrap around the end of a Dresden tool. Secure to the top of the head with edible glue. Brush a little edible glue into each of the eye sockets, make 2 small balls from Golden Bear Brown Sugar Dough and push into place. Push the end of a Black Food Colour Pen into each of the eyes.

10 Make small sections of hair at a time and build up from the back of the head, around the ears and the front of the head and up to the crown. Make small teardrops of paste, flatten and mark with a Dresden tool then secure at the wide end of the teardrop with edible glue. Curl and overlap each piece as you go.

prehistoric celebration

Once you've made your favourite dinosaurs, why not display them on a cake? Before you start this project, make sure you have all the basic items needed for covering a cake (see page 8) plus the extra edibles and equipment listed here.

edibles

15cm and 20.5cm (6" and 8") round sponge cakes

675g (1lb 7¾oz) buttercream

Jam filling (optional)

Sugarpaste: 50g (1¾oz) black, 1.25kg (2lb 12¼oz) dark green, 50g (1¾oz) teddy bear brown, 2g (pinch) white

Small amount of royal icing

SK Sugar Dough: 100g (3½oz) Green

SK Food Colour Pen: Black

SK Professional Dust Food Colours: Daffodil, Shady Moss

Cooled, boiled water

equipment

30.5cm (12") round cake drum

1m (40") x 15mm wide ribbon: gold

Bush templates (see page 56)

Paintbrushes: no. 2, 2 x no. 10 (dusting brush)

3 dowelling rods

Non-toxic glue stick

covering the cakes and drum

1 Fill the cakes with the buttercream (and jam) filling. Place the base cake onto the cake drum and cover with a thin layer of buttercream to help the sugarpaste stick.

2 Roll out 1.25kg of dark green sugarpaste on a non-stick board. Cover the whole cake and smooth over the top and sides with a smoother. Cut away any excess paste from the base of the cake with a small, sharp knife and reserve the paste.

3 Push 3 dowelling rods into the base cake for support. Mark the dowels with a Black Food Colour Pen level with the sugarpaste covering and remove from the cake. Place the dowels side-by-side on the work surface and score with a knife at the highest mark (so that they are all the same length). Snap the dowels to size and push back into the cake.

4 Cover the smaller cake in the same way as for the base cake (you do not need to dowel this cake). Spoon a small amount of royal icing

over each of the dowels and position the top cake centrally on the base cake. Smooth over the covering once again.

5 Knead the dark green sugarpaste trimmings together, roll out into a strip long enough to go around the base cake and cut a straight edge along one side. Dampen the exposed cake drum with a little cooled, boiled water and attach the strip around the base of the cake with the cut edge against the cake. Cut to size and smooth over the join with a smoother.

6 Attach the ribbon to the edge of the cake drum using a non-toxic glue stick, being careful not to come into contact with the sugarpaste.

cave

7 Roll out the black sugarpaste to a 5mm thickness, cut a straight edge at the base and a curve over the top. Attach to the side of the base cake with edible glue. Knead together the dark green trimmings and roll out a strip approximately 23cm long x 2.5cm wide. Brush edible glue over the sides of the black cave, attach the strip and cut to size at the base of the cake. Smooth over the paste with a smoother to blend it into the cake surface.

8 To make the eyeballs in the cave, divide the white sugarpaste into 4 balls, making 2 slightly larger. Shape both sets into ovals and attach in pairs inside the cave using edible glue. Mark the eyeballs and lids using a Black Food Colour Pen.

bushes

9 Knead a little white vegetable fat into the Green Sugar Dough and roll out. Cut a number of bushes in varying the sizes from the templates and set aside to dry a little. Dust over each of the bushes with Daffodil in the centre and Shady Moss around the outer edges on 1 side only. Draw a line along the inside edge of each piece using a Black Food Colour Pen. Secure some to the sides of the cake with edible glue and attach 4 to the top tier, holding in place until secure.

rocks

10 Knead and soften the teddy bear brown sugarpaste and pinch out small amounts of paste. Roll into balls and attach to the cake using edible glue. Attach rocks around the bushes on the top tier to support the bushes further.

dinosaurs

11 Attach your favourite dinosaurs to the cake and drum with edible glue to complete your design.

suppliers

Squires Kitchen, UK

3 Waverley Lane
Farnham
Surrey
GU9 8BB
0845 61 71 810
+44 1252 260 260
www.squires-shop.com

Squires Kitchen International School

The Grange
Hones Yard
Farnham
Surrey
GU9 8BB
0845 61 71 812
+44 1252 260 262
www.squires-school.co.uk

Squires Kitchen, France

www.squires-shop.fr

Squires Kitchen, Spain

www.squires-shop.es

SK stockists

Jane Asher Party Cakes
London
020 7584 6177

Blue Ribbons
Surrey
020 8941 1591

Catering Complements
Kent
01892 513745

Lawsons Ltd.
Devon
01752 892543

The Sugarcraft Emporium
Worcestershire
01527 576703

Surbiton Art & Sugarcraft
Surrey
020 8391 4664

SK distributors

Guy Paul & Co. Ltd.
Buckinghamshire
www.guypaul.co.uk

Culpitt Ltd.
Northumberland
NE63 8UQ
www.culpitt.com

manufacturers

Smeg UK Ltd.
www.smeguk.com
www.smegretro.co.uk
Italian appliance manufacturer
Smeg produces distinctive
domestic appliances combining
design, performance and quality.

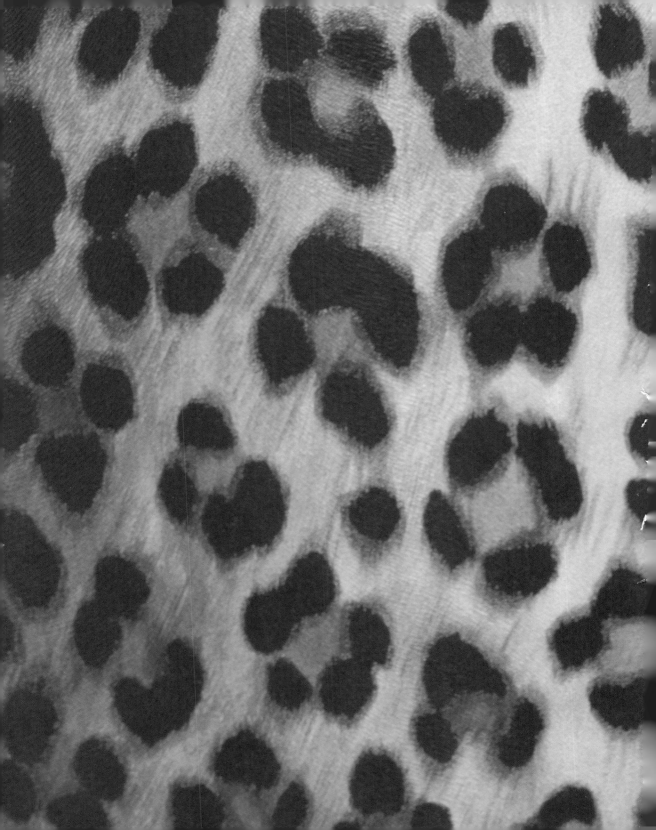